I'm Exploring with My Senses

A Song About the Five Senses

by Laura Purdie Salas

illustrated by Sergio De Giorgi

Sing along to the tune of

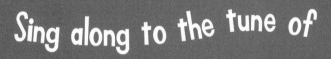

"I've Been Working on the Railroad."

Learn how your five senses help you discover the world.

The **audio file** for this book is available for **download** at:

http://www.capstonekids.com/sciencesongs

PICTURE WINDOW BOOKS
a capstone imprint

Editor: Jill Kalz
Designers: Abbey Fitzgerald and Lori Bye
Art Director: Nathan Gassman
Production Specialist: Jane Klenk
The illustrations in this book were created digitally.

Picture Window Books
151 Good Counsel Drive, P.O. Box 669
Mankato, MN 56002-0669
877-845-8392
www.picturewindowbooks.com

Printed in the United States of America in North Mankato, Minnesota.
092009
005618CGS10

All books published by Picture Window Books
are manufactured with paper containing at least
10 percent post-consumer waste.

Library of Congress Cataloging-in-Publication Data
Salas, Laura Purdie.
I'm exploring with my senses : a song about the five senses /
by Laura Purdie Salas ; illustrated by Sergio De Giorgi.
p. cm. – (Science songs)
Includes index.
ISBN 978-1-4048-5764-3 (library binding)
1. Senses and sensation–Juvenile literature. 2. Senses and
sensation–Songs and music. I. De Giorgi, Sergio, ill. II. Title.
QP434.S25 2010
612.8–dc22
2009031943

Thanks to our advisers for their expertise, research, and advice:

Jerald Dosch, Ph.D., Visiting Assistant Professor of Biology
Macalester College

Terry Flaherty, Ph.D., Professor of English
Minnesota State University, Mankato

Your five senses tell you about the world. Your eyes, ears, tongue, nose, and skin gather information and send it to your brain. Then your brain sorts it out and tells you what's going on.

Maybe you **see** pink fluff on a white stick. You **hear** no sound. You **taste** sweetness. You **smell** sugar and strawberries. The fluff **feels** soft. What is it?

All this information tells you the fluff is cotton candy. Yum! See how useful your senses are?

Grandpa brought me to the circus.

I love it so much!

I'm exploring with my senses:

Sound, sight, taste, smell, and touch.

Can't you see the sparkly costumes?

See how the trapeze flies?

I see bears and flashing cameras

When I use my eyes.

8

To see, we need light. Light enters the eye through the pupil. It's then turned into picture signals that travel to your brain. But the pictures are upside down! Your brain turns the pictures right side up and tells you what you're seeing.

Hear the drummers beat!

Hear the whistle tweet!

Hear the people laugh at clowns!

10

Tweet!!!

11

Hear the music play!

Hear the horses neigh!

My ears hear these sounds.

eardrum

When sounds enter your ear, they make your eardrum vibrate. The vibrations turn into signals. The signals then travel to your brain, and your brain tells you what the sounds are.

Lions' fur is warm and soft.

All the bars are cold, strong steel.

Cotton candy's sticky on my fingers.

This is how I think things feel.

Your skin is the largest organ in your body. Your skin lets you feel heat, cold, pressure, and pain. Nerve endings in your skin gather information about the things you touch. They send the information to your brain.

And I smell ...

Hot dogs cooking on the grill,

Smoke from the fire-eating shows.

Scents of caramel corn

And roasted peanuts fill my nose.

16

The air around us has bits of scent, or smells, in it. When you breathe in, those bits enter your nose. Nerves in your nose then send information about the smells to your brain.

Now I eat some salty popcorn.

Candy apple's tart and sweet.

Sour drops fizzle my tongue.

I'm good at finding treats to eat!

The bumps on your tongue are called papillae. They are covered with tiny taste buds. Each taste bud has a small opening that picks up flavors as food moves over it. Your brain then tells you what you're tasting. The five basic tastes are sweet, sour, salty, bitter, and umami (meaty).

So use your ...

Five senses to hear,

Smell, taste, touch, and see.

There's so much to do—

The circus is the place to be!

Did You Know?

Animals with big eyes usually see better in the dark. Their larger pupils let in more light, even when it's nighttime.

Cupping your hands around your ears does help you hear. Your cupped hands direct more sound into your ears.

Some animals smell with body parts other than their nose. Cats smell with their nose, but they also smell with the roof of their mouth! Insects smell mostly through their feelers, or antennae.

Most people have about 10,000 taste buds.

I'm Exploring with My Senses

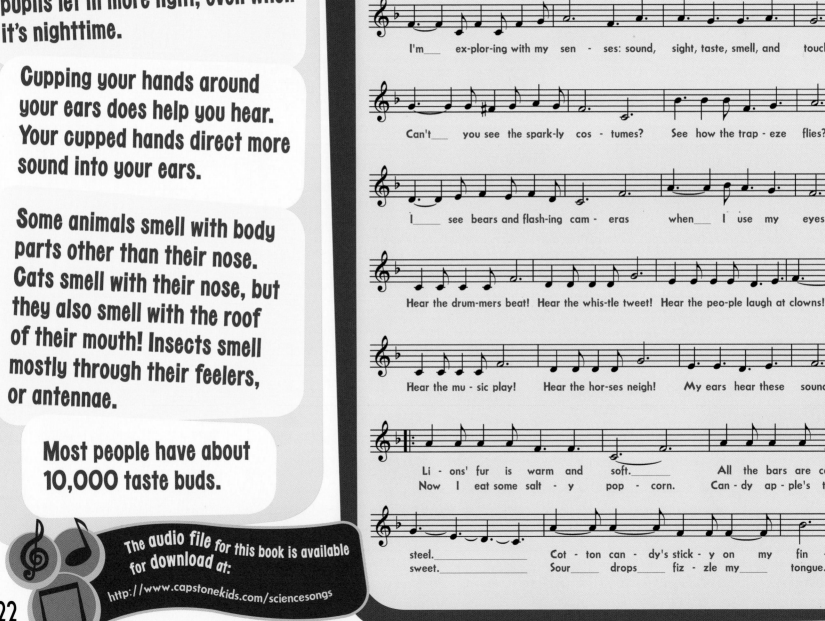

Grand - pa brought me to the cir - cus. I___ love it so much!

I'm___ ex-plor-ing with my sen - ses: sound, sight, taste, smell, and touch.

Can't___ you see the spark-ly cos - tumes? See how the trap - eze flies?

I___ see bears and flash-ing cam - eras when___ I use my eyes.

Hear the drum-mers beat! Hear the whis-tle tweet! Hear the peo-ple laugh at clowns!_____

Hear the mu - sic play! Hear the hor-ses neigh! My ears hear these sounds.

Li - ons' fur is warm and soft._____ All the bars are cold, strong
Now I eat some salt - y pop - corn. Can-dy ap-ple's tart and

steel._____ Cot - ton can - dy's stick - y on my fin - gers.
sweet._____ Sour___ drops___ fiz - zle my___ tongue. I'm

(continued from page 22)

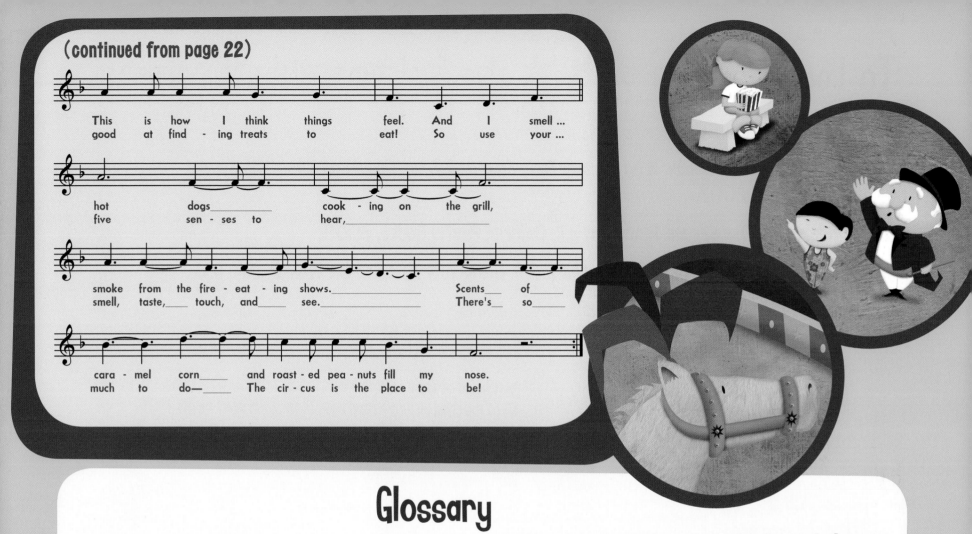

This is how I think things feel. And I smell ...
good at find - ing treats to eat! So use your ...

hot dogs_____ cook - ing on the grill,
five sen - ses to hear,_____

smoke from the fire - eat - ing shows._____ Scents___ of_____
smell, taste,____ touch, and____ see._____ There's__ so_____

cara - mel corn_____ and roast - ed pea - nuts fill my nose.
much to do—_____ The cir - cus is the place to be!

Glossary

eardrum—the thin layer of skin, or membrane, stretched across the hole inside your ear

nerve—a thread that carries messages between the brain and other parts of the body

papilla—a bump on your tongue that is covered with taste buds; *papillae* means more than one papilla.

pupil—the opening in your eye that lets in light; it looks like a black dot.

sense—one of the five powers people use to learn about their surroundings; the five senses are sight, smell, hearing, taste, and touch.

taste bud—a tiny part of your tongue that gathers information about flavors

vibrate—to move back and forth very quickly

23

To Learn More

More Books to Read

Chancellor, Deborah. *I Wonder Why Lemons Taste Sour and Other Questions About the Senses.* Boston: Kingfisher, 2007.

Ciboul, Adèle. *The Five Senses.* Richmond Hill, Ontario: Firefly Books, 2005.

Collins, Andrew. *See, Hear, Smell, Taste, and Touch: Using Your Five Senses.* Washington, D.C.: National Geographic, 2006.

Internet Sites

FactHound offers a safe, fun way to find Internet sites related to this book. All of the sites on FactHound have been researched by our staff.

Here's all you do:

Visit *www.facthound.com*

FactHound will fetch the best sites for you!

Index

brain, 3, 9, 13, 15, 17
ears, 3, 12, 13, 22, 23
eyes, 3, 8, 9, 22, 23
nerves, 15, 17
nose, 3, 16, 17, 22, 23
skin, 3, 15
taste buds, 19, 23
tongue, 3, 18, 19, 22

Look for all of the books in the Science Songs series:

♪ Are You Living?
A Song About Living and Nonliving Things

♪ Eight Great Planets!
A Song About the Planets

♪ From Beginning to End:
A Song About Life Cycles

♪ Home on the Earth:
A Song About Earth's Layers

♪ I'm Exploring with My Senses:
A Song About the Five Senses

♪ Many Creatures:
A Song About Animal Classifications

♪ Move It! Work It!
A Song About Simple Machines

♪ There Goes the Water:
A Song About the Water Cycle